HAPPY HAND
Lettering

AN INSPIRATIONAL GUIDE FOR
CREATING BEAUTIFUL WORDS OF LIFE

MAGHON TAYLOR

all she wrote notes

Published by:

P.O. Box 1010
Siloam Springs, AR 72761
dayspring.com

Written by: Maghon Taylor
Art Direction and Typeset Design by: Jessica Wei
Photography by: Megan Travis Photography
Photo on page 3: Gina Zeidler
Photo on page 142: Laura Foote Photography

Printed in China
Prime: 89898
ISBN: 978-1-68408-626-9

A NOTE FROM THE AUTHOR

Hey, y'all! I'm Maghon, and I am on a mission to help you spread happiness through your handwriting. This simple hobby has blessed me in more ways than I can even count, and my prayer is that God will use this experience to bring joy to your life in the same way He brought joy to mine.

I have been lettering as far back as I can remember—my mom even spelled my name this way because it looked prettier to write—so I think all along I was destined to be a calligrapher. I am the founder and owner of *All She Wrote Notes*, and I've taught more than seven thousand students how to hand letter through weekly hands-on workshops and even more in my online classes. Teaching is my passion, so it is my dream come true to share this skill with you!

First things first: you do *not* have to have good handwriting to have happy hand lettering.

Believe it or not, my regular handwriting is not very impressive, but when I am hand lettering, I am taken to my very own happy place. I slow down, I pay more attention, and I have *fun*. I don't get upset when I mess up, because I decided a long time ago that I can turn my mistakes into confetti—both in my lettering and my life!

I am not trained in typography, so I don't use a lot of technical terms. I am a regular girl who has carried around a bag of markers since kindergarten and I feel happiest when I'm doodling. I am going to explain lettering the same way I have taught my best girlfriends at my kitchen table, and while I won't ever say that practice makes your writing perfect, it sure does make it pretty.

You need to know that I am not a perfectionist. When I put my pen to the paper, *I am not aiming for perfection; I am aiming for joy*. When I am writing, I am thinking about the smile on someone else's face when I share my work. I am thinking of how much *joy* is in my own heart because I am taking the time to create something for fun. Whether you have big plans to share your lettering at your next dinner party, or you're planning on making some fun birthday cards or a happy sticky note for your favorite coworker, or you plan to Bible journal to your heart's content—*you* have the power to make someone happier with your handwriting.

In my personal life, happiness is the ultimate goal. I work hard to create happy moments, memories, and experiences for myself and for our family, but I also make a conscious effort every single day to speak positive words, to practice gratitude, and to do at least one little thing that brings me joy. When our cup is full, we can't help but overflow God's love to those around us, and Happy Hand Lettering is one of my favorite ways to pour out joy to others.

Our words can change our world. They matter. And as you work your way through each lesson in this book, I hope you accept these beautiful words of life and see how they apply directly to you. Each of the quotes and Scriptures is meant to encourage and inspire you. Every project contains practical lettering advice and tips, but also includes ideas for little ways to make your *life* happier, too. My prayer is to leave you feeling lighter, more inspired, more creative, and of course even happier than you are right now.

Thank you for giving yourself this gift of time—this slice of your day to do something creative, to feel inspired, to connect to God's Word, maybe in a way you haven't before. I am so proud that you're doing something fun for *you*! You deserve it.

We are going to have so much fun!

Love,

TABLE OF CONTENTS

SECTION 5

*If you don't speak the "lettering language," don't worry!
I created a glossary for you in the back of the book—
so if you run into a **bolded** word that doesn't make sense to you,
you can flip to the back to find its meaning.

WHAT IS HAND LETTERING?

MY INTRODUCTION TO HAND LETTERING

When I was a little girl I visited a local gift store called Animal Quackers, and in my young mind the girl working there had the *coolest* job! Once I picked out my favorite bookbag, pencil case, or lunch box, it was her job to use a paint marker and write my name permanently on the supplies! Officially making them mine and only mine. She used an all-caps style first and then went back through to add big polka dots to the corner of each capital letter. But that wasn't all! Then she took a second color of marker and added a tiny accent dot to each of the big dots, sending my little mind into overdrive. I was absolutely mesmerized by the beauty. I couldn't even contain how much I loved it. She used her handwriting to make little Maghon as happy as a nineties kid could be.

My mom knew how much I loved this style and soon began to purchase the markers and teach herself how to hand letter. It was a different style back then but with the very same purpose—to make regular handwriting happy enough to bless someone else. She would use this style on my brown paper lunch bags, my envelope that contained my birthday card, and on gift tags that we gave to other friends. I've never forgotten how it looked or, most importantly, how it made me feel.

Isn't that something? Such a little thing, such an ordinary thing, that can have a beautiful impact. I believe that God can use the little things in life to bring us joy. I have no doubt God is an artist! He didn't have to use all the pretty colors for flowers, but aren't you so glad He did? And a sunset?! Holy smokes, that pink, that blue, that orange! All the many blues of the ocean... I could go on, but you get the point. I can think of a thousand examples in nature where God added color because He was probably like, "Hey, this looks like fun!" I think He uses ordinary things like our handwriting to bring us joy. And not only to us, but to the other people we encounter. These ordinary things are most certainly gifts when we choose to celebrate them and see them this way.

THE DEFINITION
OF HAND LETTERING

As previously mentioned, my regular handwriting is not all that impressive. When I make a grocery list or a thank-you note, I'm usually in a hurry. I am scribbling on scrap paper with whatever pen I can find and aiming for function, not fun. When I sign my receipt at our favorite taco joint, it looks just like yours—a bunch of squiggles. Hold on, though. Don't close the book just yet! When I sit down to hand letter, I go about it in a completely different way. You do *not* have to have good handwriting to have happy hand lettering.

You do not have to have good Handwriting to have

HAPPY HAND Lettering

I like to think that *hand lettering is a happier version of ordinary handwriting.* Hand lettering is more intentional, more embellished, more fun, and more creative than your grocery-list script. **Hand lettering** is a lot more like drawing than it is writing. Hand lettering elevates ordinary **handwriting** from drab to fab.

WHAT IS THE DIFFERENCE BETWEEN HAND LETTERING AND CALLIGRAPHY?

Calligraphy is most often done with an old-fashioned metal nib dipped into a jar of ink. Don't panic; that isn't what we are doing here. But I lovingly refer to hand lettering as "Fauxlligraphy." Basically, when we are hand lettering, we are faking calligraphy with a marker instead of a nib. I am trained as a calligrapher, and I love and practice the art regularly, but I like to say that hand lettering is calligraphy's casual little sister. Hand lettering definitely favors her older sis in appearance (with thick and thin lines), but she is more laid-back, more versatile, and more accessible since supplies are so much easier to come by and often easier to use.

Instead of using a metal-tipped pen, hand lettering can be achieved with any pointed marker or drawing tool. Hand lettering is not pressure-sensitive like calligraphy. Instead, we will draw letter shapes in the **monoline** style that naturally comes out of the pen when we write. You don't have to hold the pen any certain way or sit in a different posture. Instead we write each of our regular letters (with a couple of tips from me!), and then we will go back and apply **downstrokes** and **shading** to mimic calligraphy.

Due to the nature of the tools as well as how we choose to infuse our own unique styles, hand lettering tends to look more casual than pointed-pen calligraphy...but you can make it as formal or as simple as you choose. Your style is as versatile as the clothes in your closet!

Handwriting is a white T-shirt.
Hand lettering is your favorite party outfit.
Calligraphy is an elegant ball gown.

HAND LETTERING TIPS

Here are my best tips for hand lettering
and how it's different from my regular handwriting.

HAND LETTERING IS NOT QUICK!

For starters, I slow down.

Although you will definitely pick up the pace as your skills improve, good stuff takes time. Hand lettering an envelope takes me three times as long as if I were writing it with a regular ink pen in my grocery-list script. But it is at least a hundred times more beautiful, so I think it's definitely worth it!

HAND LETTERING
IS NOT *QUITE*
THE SAME AS CURSIVE

These letters definitely have cursive vibes and roots, but they take on traits from *your* style and penmanship. Your alphabet can be more or less formal than cursive depending on your intentions. *You* have complete artistic control and expression. See where this takes you. Sometimes letters just have a personality of their own!

Most importantly, when you're hand lettering, *most of the letters are not connected* to one another. Instead, you'll write each letter one at a time, and they overlap each other. They will look like they were connected all in one swoop, like when we sign our names, but it's actually the opposite. The letters were drawn individually. That is great news for us, because we only have to be good at one letter at a time. All the praise hands!

When I hand letter, I am much more intentional about the way I make letters, how they look, and how they are placed so they can connect to one another.

HAND LETTERING IS NOT A FONT; IT IS A TECHNIQUE

More great news! There is not *one* exclusive alphabet guide to follow for your writing to be considered hand lettering. There is not *only* one way to write each letter! Instead, there is a three-step technique that I apply to each of my ordinary letters to transform them into my happy hand lettering. We all have different swoops and loops, entrances and exits, that make our handwriting styles unique. We each may have our own versions of the letters. I never want to take those away from you; instead, I want to help you celebrate what makes your penmanship style different and perfect it to look even better! You will find alphabet guides throughout this book—my favorite versions of letters I use every day. But I don't want your creativity to be reined in by those. I made them up! Use these alphabets as inspiration to develop your own unique style. There are hundreds and thousands of ways you can write A–Z. If my style doesn't fit your personality, you can use my three-step technique to help you develop your own that feels like a happier version of your ordinary handwriting.

HAND LETTERING
IS NOT SMALL

If you write as tiny as the tooth fairy does, we are going to have some problems! I am going to challenge you to write *big* while you are learning to hand letter. I write at least 1"-1.5" tall, depending on the project. Of course once you've got this down, you can make your lettering as big or as small as you want to—as big as a poster board or as small as a gift tag—but for now, let's aim big so that there's plenty of room in between letters to add shading to our downstrokes.

1 inch tall!

1.5 inches tall!

LET'S PRACTICE!

Write your name 1 inch tall.

Now write your name 1.5 inches tall.

WHEN IN DOUBT, FLUFF IT OUT!

Hand lettering is not skinny. My favorite rule to share is "When in doubt, **fluff it out!**" What this means is that in order for your handwriting to become hand lettering, you need to loosen up your letters so there's room for the thick and thin lines. If you write in a rigid style or draw the letters super tight and close together, adding thick lines will entirely overtake your letters, and you'll be left with blobs of ink. Not to mention, you'll most certainly be disappointed. Fluff out your ordinary cursive to transform it into happy hand lettering.

And one more…

KEEP THE PARTY GOING!

In order to turn ordinary handwriting into hand lettering, there is one major modification that has to be made. Each letter must be extended forward to be able to connect to future letters. We can't just stop at the bottom of a letter; instead, **keep the party going**. When you're almost done writing a letter, continue the **stroke** forward and at an upward angle—almost like saying "ta da!" with a smile. Go up like a smile, not down like a frown. After all, this is *happy* hand lettering.

Keeping the party going makes each letter prepped and ready to high-five and connect to whatever letter is coming next. If you stop short and drop the baton…you're not being a good teammate, and you're literally leaving the rest of the word hanging. You need to make sure you've extended that hand for the cleanest and easiest overlap when you're ready to connect letters.

When in doubt, fluff it out. Practice loosening up your cursive letters below.

Let's keep the party going and practice overlapping letters.

FAVORITE SUPPLIES

SETUP

One of my favorite things about hand lettering is that it can be done absolutely anywhere! We don't have to be at a table or desk, although of course we can! But I most often hand letter in my lap. You can write straight into this book (and I hope you will)! But I also love having a clipboard or lap desk handy so that I can letter while I am comfy on my couch. If it's a larger project, I take it straight to the floor and spread out so I can get up close and personal to the poster board or chalkboard sign. Don't wait until you have the perfect setup; you already have everything you need to get started today!

SUPPLIES

My other favorite thing is that hand lettering supplies are *so* easy to find. You probably already own lots of writing tools that will work great for hand lettering. I don't believe that we have to have expensive tools to make our handwriting beautiful. We can hand letter with a pencil, a crayon, or whatever pointed-tip tool is lying around, but my ultimate favorite is a new, fresh, pointed-tip marker, like a Sharpie™.

Once the marker has run out of ink or the tip is no longer pointed, that's all she wrote! I joke that that's no longer a Sharpie; that's a "dully," and there's no magic left in a magic marker that doesn't write. Hand lettering always works best with juicy, sharp, newish markers that still have a lot left to say.

Here are some of my all-time favorite brands and supplies that I use daily:

- Sharpie Fine Point
- Sharpie Flip Chart
- Crayola™ Super Tips
- Crayola Classic Broad Point Markers
- Sharpie Paint Markers
- Pilot™ Gold Paint Pen
- Pentouch® Gold + Silver Paint Pen

The most important rule when shopping for hand lettering supplies is that you want to get a pointed or rounded tip. Never buy a "calligraphy marker" or even a "brush-tip marker" for this job. The marker should have a sharp or rounded point to give the most control during lettering and shading.

I don't use super-skinny markers or gel pens often because a marker covers more ground in less time. As you'll find, a gel pen or a super-skinny marker takes longer to add shading to your downstrokes, but when I am lettering in my planner or needing to write something smaller, these are my go-to tools:

- Uni-ball Signo Gel Ink pens (bold). Love these in white, silver, and gold.
- Paper Mate™ Inkjoy pens
- Marvy Uchida Le Pen™
- Staedtler™ pens
- Pentel™ Flair pens (come in allll the colors)
- Micron™ pens
- Sharpie Extra Fine Point marker

PAPER

As for paper, if I am practicing, I simply use computer paper or a sturdy sketchbook. If I am making something to sell or to gift, I use heavyweight card stock. You can buy it in white or in *all* the fun colors (my personal fave!).

DIGITAL

I am a paper-and-pen gal for life, but I really enjoy doodling for fun on my iPad®! I have the iPad Pro® and use the Procreate® app for lettering. I love how easy it is to practice on there with the Apple® pencil. I find that I am still much better (and more precise) with old-fashioned paper and pen, but it's fun to be able to take my skills on the go! This also saves a step if you want to digitize lettering for print. I sometimes use iPad doodles for fun quotes on Instagram or to make vinyl stickers with my hand lettering that I can then cut out with my Silhouette or any smart die-cutting machine. Lots of letterers use iPad doodles to make designs for T-shirts and coffee mugs...but if I have the choice, I still prefer old-fashioned paper and pen.

TIPS FOR PRACTICE

The best way to get better at writing is by *writing*! This may seem counterintuitive, but if you practice your letters first and build a strong foundation with those, then you will see a drastic improvement in your words—especially since the words are all drawn one letter at a time. Some of my favorite drills are to write a full page of the same letter, with different versions and modifications each time. This is a great challenge to not only stretch your creativity but to stretch your skills, as well!

When I am practicing words, my favorite things to write are people's names. It's instant gratification, because people *love* their names. I especially like to take a photo of my friend's hand-lettered name and text it to her. You should try it! I guarantee that she is going to write back with all the heart eyes!

TURN YOUR mistakes
INTO confetti.

ALLSHEWROTENOTES.COM

THE
PROCESS

JOY, NOT PERFECTION

I am not a perfectionist. Not that there's anything wrong with being one—both Jesus and I still love you if you are—but I feel like you should know that about me right out of the gate. I framed my son Vance's first Sharpie drawing on our kitchen wall; I am known to subscribe to Bob Ross's philosophy of "happy accidents"; and I turn all my mistakes into **confetti**.

When I put my pen to the paper, I am not aiming for perfection; I am aiming for *joy*. I am focused on having fun, enjoying the process, and feeling creative and inspired. I get lost in my doodling. It actually relaxes me because I am so focused on it that all my other worries tend to fall away. If I am making something to give away, I think about the joy it will bring the recipient—the way their eyes will light up when they see their name beautifully written out or the way their heart will feel, knowing that I made something just for them.

I would like to invite you to adopt this philosophy in your lettering journey, as well. Don't get too caught up in trying to make every letter perfect. Just make it look happy! Your work will always be viewed as a whole word or paragraph, not individual letters, and you will probably be your own worst critic. Tiny imperfections don't take away from the art itself. In fact, I think it makes the piece even more special because it's clear that you made it by hand. It doesn't have to be perfect to be beautiful. So let's get this party started!

A THREE-STEP PROCESS

My happy hand lettering technique is made up of three steps.

STEP 1

Draw the letter, and draw it big.

STEP 2

Add parallel lines next to your downstrokes to thicken them out.

STEP 3

Shade/color in between the original letter and the downstroke line.

Otherwise known as—*draw the letter, add the line, and shade it in!*

STEP 1: DRAW THE LETTER

As I mentioned before, hand lettering is not quite like cursive. The letters will look as if they are connected, but they are actually drawn one by one and will overlap each other. Ninety percent of the letters you'll draw in hand lettering are written all by themselves.

You'll want to write big so that you have plenty of room for your upstrokes and downstrokes. I challenge you to write at least 1"-1.5" high for practice. Don't forget to implement your happy hand lettering tips (when in doubt, fluff it out and keep the party going).

Note: You don't need to re-learn how to write all your letters. I've had so many students ask me, "Maghon, how do you write an *a*?" and my reply is always "You know how to write an *a*—you learned that in elementary school, girl!" You see, in hand lettering, all you're doing is taking what you already know how to do, and adapting it.

This first step is the easiest, but take your time. Don't rush through letter placement, and keep in mind that you're laying down the letters one at a time and they are overlapping one another. It is fine if they cross over and don't connect perfectly, because Step 2 is on the way to save the day!

Step One is not very impressive *yet*. Sometimes my students have even described this step as messy-looking, awkward, or the letters appear too loose. Keep going. You don't have to rewrite Step One a hundred times until it is perfect, because it won't look its best until you've completed Steps Two and Three. You will see major improvements when you add those! You won't even believe it's the same handwriting. It's like when you get out of the shower and your hair is still wet. Who *is* that girl? There's probably some work left to do before you're 100 percent confident about leaving the house—at least for me, that's the case. Let's blow-dry and style, shall we?

a b c d e f
g h i j k l
m n o p q
r s t u v w
x y z

Trace this phrase.

Now draw your own!

STEP 2: ADD THE LINE

lines a a a

The most important piece of hand lettering is being able to determine the difference between an **upstroke** and a **downstroke**.

Let's start with the letter *a*, for example. Humor me for a minute—I want you to draw your lowercase cursive *a* with your finger in the air. Do it now; I am watching. Don't read on until you've drawn the *a* in the air, or you're going to think I am not making any sense. When we draw the letter *a*, we go down, up, down, and then back up at the end, when we keep the party going. Step Two is all about determining where the downstrokes are.

Anytime the hand comes back toward the body or down toward the bottom of the paper... that's a downstroke. Anytime the hand moves up and away from the body or toward the top of the paper...that's an upstroke. The goal with hand lettering is to make downstrokes thick and keep upstrokes thin.

When we are happily hand lettering, we are going to give all the love and attention to the downstrokes and leave the upstrokes just as they are, in the same width they come out of the pen.

After you draw each letter, or once you've completed a word, go back through and trace the direction of each letter with your finger. This is where we will refresh our memory as to which parts are the downstrokes and which parts are upstrokes.

If you are ever stumped when hand lettering and feel confused about which part to thicken and shade, trace back over that letter with your finger or draw it in the air. Toward you is a downstroke; away from you is an upstroke. Downstrokes are thick, and upstrokes are thin.

Once you've located the downstrokes, you will want to add a second line that is parallel to the downstroke. It should taper along the same shape as the letter—from the highest point to the lowest point—but no farther.

Do you add shading to the left side or the right side of the downstroke?

This is the most common question I get asked when teaching. Want to hear some great news? It doesn't matter! You want to go where you have the most room and where it will look the best. This can differ from letter to letter, so either side works. Your goal is simply to thicken the stroke and make it wider.

Most of the time, I naturally add shading to the right of the original line, but if there is a circular letter like an *o*, it looks best when shading is done on the inside of the shape rather than the outside. Pick a side, any side!

You will want that downstroke line to taper along the shape of the letter as you draw.

You will apply downstrokes to your word letter by letter. This is the most important—and most commonly missed—step in hand lettering. Be careful not to skip ahead to Step Three once you become more experienced, because this is the step that makes your writing look uniform and polished.

Depending on the size of your marker, lots of times Steps One and Two will do a lot of the work for you. You could even stop after Steps One and Two and have a fun and unique happy-hand-lettering style with just the letters and the lines, but keep going to Step Three for the full faux-lligraphy effect.

I like to compare this step to blow-drying your hair. It's not soaking wet then; you can throw it into a ponytail or a messy bun and call it a day—and, believe me, lots of days I do! You can drop the mic and be done here...but if you really want to wow and take it to the next level, then you'll want to add some style!

Trace and add the downstroke lines to this alphabet.

a b c d e f

g h i j k l

m n o p q

r s t u v w

x y z

Trace and add the downstroke lines to this phrase.

Now draw your own and add the lines!

STEP 3: SHADE IT IN!

shading *a a a*

The third and final step in happy hand lettering is where you really bring your handwriting from drab to fab.

You've drawn your letters (Step One); you've added lines next to your downstrokes (Step Two); and here in Step Three, you're going to shade in the gaps!

You will use the tip of your marker to fill in the gap between your original letter and your second line. Now, here's where you've got to be careful. This isn't kindergarten coloring (as much fun as that sounds, there's no scribbling allowed). I like to use my marker tip as if I'm highlighting *one* small verse in my Bible. I use long, clean, and smooth strokes from top to bottom instead of a hundred tiny feathered brushstrokes. Be careful not to scribble back and forth when you're shading or sketch/feather in the color like you're Bob Ross painting Happy Trees. We are going for refined, not rugged. Deal?

I love using markers, because you get the most bang for your buck! It is much faster to color with a pointed tip marker than it is with a gel pen. You can actually turn your marker to the side and use that pointed tip to lay down smooth, bold color that looks neat and tidy.

Lots of times, depending on the size of your marker, Steps One and Two will do most of the work and you just barely have to fill in holes with Step Three, but your goal is to finish each letter with a bold, thick downstroke and maintain the thin upstrokes just as they are.

Now you're looking fresh! If you make it all the way to shading your letters, you will see major improvement in how your hand lettering looks and feels. It is most certainly a happier version of your regular handwriting.

And back to my hairstyling example...when you've taken your hairstyle to the next level, you're more confident and bold and shining happier than before.

Trace and shade in the downstrokes in this alphabet.

a b c d e f
g h i j k l
m n o p q
r s t u v w
x y z

Trace and shade the downstrokes in this phrase.

shade it IN

shade it IN

Now draw your own letters, add the line, and shade it in!

Yay! You did it! Great job!

ENCOURAGEMENT AND REFLECTION

Take a second to look back to where you started. See how your letters have improved from your regular handwriting to learning the modifications you needed for hand lettering. You've gotten so much better in just a few minutes. Take note of the drastic appearance improvements between Steps One, Two, and Three. It only takes a few extra minutes, but turning ordinary handwriting into happy hand lettering really makes a difference. You are doing awesome!

PRACTICE PAGES

Use these pages to practice your alphabet in cursive. We may all have different versions of each letter, but that's okay! They can *all* be used for hand lettering. Remember, hand lettering is not a **font**; it's a technique, so you can apply my three steps to any of your handwriting. Plus, by remembering to fluff it out (see page 20) and keep the party going (see page 21), you'll be hand lettering in no time.

MY FAVORITE ALPHABET

Early on in the beginning stages of my company, All She Wrote Notes, I was not very good at lettering, but that never stopped me from enjoying every minute. I was having so much fun, and it was so refreshing to be creative for a change. Calligraphy was my hobby when I got home after my 9-to-5 event-planning job. I loved my job, but I was always on a computer screen and I missed being creative. I missed crafting, drawing, painting, and making a big mess. I have always enjoyed crafting for friends, so I took a set of handwritten note cards to my book club for hostess gifts. My friend Laura said, "I've never seen calligraphy look so *fun*!"

Now, I don't think she meant to change my life with that compliment, but God will sometimes put people into your life at the exact right time. She had no way of knowing that I was feeling like I wasn't good enough. Or that I was comparing my writing to other professional lettering artists online and thinking mine wasn't elegant enough, formal enough, or perfect enough to ever "make it." But when she said it looked *fun*, it was like a whole new world of possibility opened to me. Nobody has ever called me *elegant* a day in my life, but *fun*... Let's just say that I'm the life of the party!

It was at that moment that everything changed. I stopped comparing myself to everybody else and kept my eyes on my own paper. God made me *me*, so why should I try to be like anyone else? My handwriting didn't have to be formal or fancy. I didn't need perfect penmanship to make her day! I could just be me, and that was enough! It was with Laura's encouraging words that I found the confidence to start sharing my happy hand lettering online, and the rest is history—or HIS story. God had a plan to use my talents that was far greater than anything I could have imagined.

This is my favorite alphabet, which I use daily when I am hand lettering. The lowercase letter forms are simpler and easier to read but can easily be embellished and accessorized depending on the project. If you're looking to dress up your current writing or there's a letter that is leaving you stumped, adopt a few of my letters and make them your own. I will share the letters for you to practice and also some tips and additional thoughts along the way.

a b c d e

f g h i j

k l m n n

56

o p q r

s t u v w

x y z

LETTER BY LETTER
WITH INSTRUCTION

Vowels: *a, e, i, o, u*

We will start here since these are letters you already know and use every single day! Your vowels are not where you want to get creative. No matter how beautiful your lettering looks, if they can't read your vowels, they will have no idea what you are trying to say. I keep these as simple and as clean as possible and save the **flourishes** and **embellishments** for future letters. Remember to keep the party going at the end of each letter so that it can easily be connected to future letters to form words.

| LET'S PRACTICE! | Draw a vowel, add the line, and shade it in. |

e e e

Also similar to vowels and very simple to write: *c, v, w*

Draw the letter, add the line, and shade it in.

Did you notice how a lot of the alphabet is made up of similar shapes? For example, the rounded circle shape that starts a, d, and g, or the way h and n are basically the same except for different heights—or the way lowercase i and t both go straight down first and then up?

Letters r, s, x, and z are all unique because they start with an upstroke (instead of a downstroke), and it's actually easier to connect them like cursive when you're writing instead of stopping in between.

Lots of this is muscle memory, and the more you letter and develop your own style, the more you'll pick up on these similarities and others.

TIME FOR A BOGO DEAL

When you're hand lettering, you want to make sure that each letter has at least one thick and one thin line. To help achieve the thick-and-thin balance in my alphabet, I add a **BOGO**! Because who doesn't love a BOGO deal—a buy one, get one free sale? I am so there! When I am making modifications to my ordinary grocery-list script for hand lettering, the first thing I remember is "When in doubt, fluff it out"! Here's the easiest way for me to do that. Anywhere there is initially a straight line (for example, the right side of an *a* or the left side of a *b*), I will instead add an upstroke *and* a downstroke. I call this motion a BOGO! You'll notice the BOGO motion a lot in my regular alphabet. It's basically one of my greatest hits.

Here are letters that would totally love a BOGO deal: *a, b, d, f, h, k, m, n*

Try out some letters that can add a BOGO.

LET'S PRACTICE!

ASCENDERS

In addition to the *b*, *d*, *h*, and *k* in our previous section, these letters all have their party at the top, meaning that the letters are ascenders. When you write these four, your marker starts at the **midline**, swoops down, and then swings back up to the top.

f, *l*, *p*–"When in doubt, fluff it out." If you keep the loops too tightly together or too skinny, then your downstroke will flood your shape.

If you have two letters back to back, you don't have to pick up your pen; you can just roll from one letter right into the next letter. They don't have to be exact replicas, either. It is even okay if your two *l*'s have slightly different shapes–they can be sisters; they don't have to be twins!

I love hand-lettered art even more for this very reason. You can see imperfections! Don't hide them; be proud of them! They mean that your work is handmade, handwritten, one of a kind, unique, original, limited edition, and straight from the heart.

LET'S PRACTICE!   Write "hello" below and fluff it out!

The *t* is my favorite letter in this category! Add fun and flare to your *t* with the cross. You can go as creative or as simple as you prefer, but I *love* adding a big swooping cross to my lowercase *t*. With my last name being Taylor, I actually prefer to write it with a lowercase *t* instead of a capital.

The important thing to note with your lowercase *t* is that the downstroke is shaded thickly but the cross is not. The cross is your thin line, so it's acting as your upstroke. You want each letter to have at least one downstroke and one upstroke. Even if you make a downward motion in your cross, it looks better to break the rule and leave it thin.

When there are two *t*'s back to back, like in the word *confetti*, I like to tackle them both together with a single swooping cross instead of two separate ones that are squished next to each other.

Trace "confetti" below and then try crossing some *t*'s.

DESCENDERS

Descenders usually start in the middle and then drop below the baseline. I call this having their party at the bottom. These are fun to write because they can be dressed up or down, simple or fancy, and can really showcase your own penmanship personality. Look at how many different ways you can draw these letters. Have fun stretching your creativity.

LET'S PRACTICE!   Try drawing the letters *g*, *j*, and *p* below

Letters *q* and *p* can be written so many different ways, with variable **entrances** and **exits**. I grew up as a dancer, and during every recital my teacher would stress the importance of how to walk onstage and how to walk offstage. It was almost as important as how I performed. With these letters, there are lots of options for how to bring them onstage and how to walk them off.

Try drawing the letters *q* and *y* below.

LET'S PRACTICE!

r s s x z

Letters *r*, *s*, *x*, and *z* begin with an upstroke. It's actually easier to write them in cursive and connect them to previous letters than to stop in between letters like we usually do with hand lettering.

extra

extra

extra

cheers

cheers

cheers

ADVANCED ALPHABETS: SIGNATURE SWIRL

Now, if you are looking to spice up the original letters, I've got you, girl! This alphabet is called my Signature Swirl (aka my alFUNbet).

This style is made up of curly and swirly letters, most of which I use today! When I am lettering in this style, I don't curl every single letter, just as I don't wear every bracelet I own at once. In this case, less is more. I usually swirl out the entrance and exit letters and maybe one in the middle, if I am feeling fancy. Have fun with them—though this may be the one and only time I'll tell you to rein it in. If you try to swirl every letter, it will look like the fairy godmother wrote a ransom note.

a b c d e

f g h i j

k l m n

O P R B R

S T U V

W X Y Z

A B C D

E F G H

I J K L

M N O
P Q R S
T U V W
X Y Z

EMBELLISHMENTS

BASELINE VARIANCES

Vary the **baseline**. You can make your letters **bounce**! Can you hear the change in your tone when you read bounce #1 vs. bounce #2? Which one looks more formal? Which one looks more fun? When you lay the letters down one by one, you can vary the baseline by making some of your letters higher and some of your letters lower. This is just one of many ways you can add personality to your penmanship.

FLOURISH

I add swirls and curls to the front and back of words to make them fancier and more formal. I call these entrances and exits. Every once in a while, I will swirl out a *g* or a *y* in the middle of a word to keep things interesting.

NUMBERS

I like to keep my numbers simple and readable, because if the post office can't tell in two seconds whether it's a 1 or a 7, my love letter won't make it to its intended destination. When using numbers on something that won't be mailed (like table numbers, for example), then the more the merrier when it comes to embellishments and swirls.

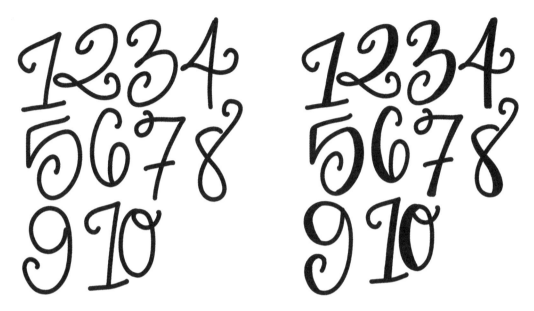

PUNCTUATION

I never want the punctuation to take away from the word itself, so I follow my rules of making the downstrokes thick and the upstrokes thin, always striving to maintain that thick-and-thin balance on each letter or mark.

PRINT vs. script

Hand lettering is a technique, not a **font**—meaning that there's not *only* one way to write each letter. You can come up with a dozen different letter *A*'s and they will all work for hand lettering.

Hand lettering is also not only for cursive writing! The same techniques can be applied to print writing as well. With one exception. When you are thickening downstrokes on print letters, thicken the first downstroke you see but then keep it moving, sister! One and done. The reason for this is because some print letters are written with all downstroke motions, and every letter should have that thick-and-thin balance.

I always use this **block font** when I make something for my husband or son, as they don't seem to appreciate the curls and swirls as much as I do!

A B C D E
F G H I J K
L M N O P
Q R S T U
V W X Y Z

abcdef
ghijklm
nopqrst
uvwxyz

Try some hand lettering in a print style!

TIPS ON HOW TO CHANGE IT UP

Just when you get comfortable practicing the basics of hand lettering, it's time to switch it up (I've got to keep you on your toes!). In the next few pages, I will share some of my favorite ways to get *even more* creative with hand lettering. These tips will stretch your creativity in new ways and will help you look at letters differently. You may even ask yourself how you could change up your ordinary style and try something new.

When you're hand lettering, you have the option to draw just the letters, draw the letters plus the lines, or do all three steps to shade it in for the faux-lligraphy effect. ANY of these styles count as happy hand lettering!

AΛEƐHHKK

MMPPPRRtt

DIFFERENT PROPORTIONS

BBℬℬ gₒg

MⱮ jj

yy y ʒ

MIXING FONTS

mix it up

I love to mix up fonts and use **script** and **block fonts** together. This helps emphasize important words and convey my message in a clearer way. It is also a little faster and easier to read.

IN THIS HOUSE WE *serve* THE *Lord*

TODAY is
A
GOOD
Day FOR
baby
THE
Joy
WORK Hard
Stay sweet
Love Deep

PROJECTS

BEAUTIFUL WORDS OF LIFE

The two questions I get asked most are:

1. Can you show me how to write like that?
2. How are you always so happy?

The answer to number one is: *I sure can!* I am *so* glad you asked. I have this book called *Happy Hand Lettering*. Oh, what's that? You're reading it now? Well, don't let me interrupt you.

But for question number two, I've given it a lot of thought over the years. I don't think there's one specific thing that makes me happier than the average person; I think it's a lot of little things that added up. I haven't always had the easiest of circumstances, and I've been through more struggles than I can count...but I realized a long time ago that God gives me joy even in my darkest moments. I try my best to fully recognize and appreciate His goodness no matter what is happening in my life. I actually believe it's because of my hardest days that I can fully appreciate and honor the good times and happy moments as they are happening. I am SO grateful to be happy, because I haven't forgotten how it feels to be sad.

When I was in high school (one of many hard seasons) I carried around a quote book of motivational messages, each one hand lettered with bright markers and positive energy. Some were song lyrics, some were Bible verses, and some were quotes I came across and illustrated so I wouldn't ever forget them. I remember taking my trusty quote book with me to college (yet another trying time for my heart and my faith), and I clung to that notebook as I referenced it for important life moments such as creating my Myspace profile and AIM "away" messages. A few years later, those quotes found their way into Facebook status updates and tweets on Twitter. As social media began to work its way into my world, I found I could share these quotes with so many people! And before I knew it, I was sharing joy with more than thirty thousand people every single day through Pinterest, Instagram, and many different social media platforms.

As we work our way through the next fourteen projects, I want to share lessons on lettering—but I also want to share my lessons on life. These beautiful words of life are some of my favorite quotes and, more importantly, my favorite lessons on *how* to live a happier life. Words matter, and if we can change the way we talk to each other, to ourselves, and even to God, our lives can change for the better. I never pretend to be an expert on either lettering or life—far from it—but what I'm going to share are things that drastically impact my mood, lift my spirits, and allow me to be a light for others and for myself. This is what puts the "happy" in my Happy Hand Lettering, and my prayer is that these projects will help add more happiness to your life too.

²⁸ for dominion belongs to the LORD
and he rules over the nations.

²⁹ All the rich of the earth will feast and
worship;
all who go down to the dust will
before him—
those who cannot keep themselves
alive.

³⁰ Posterity will serve him;
future generations will be told about
the Lord.

³¹ They will proclaim his righteousness,
declaring to a people yet unborn:
He has done it!

8/17

Psalm 23

A psalm of David.

¹ The LORD is my shepherd, I lack
nothing.

² He makes me lie down in green
pastures,
he leads me beside quiet waters,

³ he refreshes my soul.
He guides me along the right paths
for his name's sake.

⁴ Even though I walk
through the darkest valley,
I will fear no evil,
for you are with me;
your rod and your staff,
they comfort me.

⁵ You prepare a table before me
in the presence of my enemies.
You anoint my head with oil;
my cup overflows.

⁶ Surely your goodness and love will follow
me
all the days of my life,
and I will dwell in the house of the LORD
forever.

REMEMBER
I LACK NOTHING
I shall not want
Bad times + Good
NO FEAR

Psalm 24

Of David. A psalm.

¹ The earth is the LORD's, and everything
in it,
the world, and all who live in it;

² for he founded it on the seas
and established it on the waters.

³ Who may ascend the mountain of the
LORD?
Who may stand in his holy place?

⁴ The one who has clean hands and a pure
heart,
who does not trust in an idol
or swear by a false god.

⁵ They will receive blessing from the LORD
and vindication from God their Savior.

⁶ Such is the generation of those who seek
him,
who seek your face, God of Jacob.

⁷ Lift up your heads, you gates;
be lifted up, you ancient doors,
that the King of glory may come in.

⁸ Who is this King of glory?
The LORD strong and mighty,
the LORD mighty in battle.

⁹ Lift up your heads, you gates;
lift them up, you ancient doors,
that the King of glory may come in.

¹⁰ Who is he, this King of glory?
The LORD Almighty—
he is the King of glory.

← GRATEFUL FOR THIS

Psalm 25

Of David.

¹ In you, LORD my God,
I put my trust.

² I trust in you;
do not let me be put to shame,
nor let my enemies triumph over me.

³ No one who hopes in you
will ever be put to shame,
but shame will come on those
who are treacherous without cause.

⁴ Show me your ways, LORD,
teach me your paths.

⁵ Guide me in your truth and teach me,
for you are God my Savior,
and my hope is in you all day long.

⁶ Remember, LORD, your great mercy and
love,
for they are from of old.

---

⁷ Do not remember the sins of my youth
and my rebellious ways;
according to your love remember me,
for you, LORD, are good.

⁸ Good and upright is the LORD;
therefore he instructs sinners in his
ways.

⁹ He guides the humble in what is right
and teaches them his way.

¹⁰ All the ways of the LORD are loving and
faithful
toward those who keep the demands of
his covenant.

¹¹ For the sake of your name, LORD,
forgive my iniquity, though it is great.

¹² Who, then, are those who fear the LORD?
He will instruct them in the ways they
should choose.

¹³ They will spend their days in prosperity,
and their descendants will inherit the
land.

¹⁴ The LORD confides in those who fear
him;
he makes his covenant known to them.

¹⁵ My eyes are ever on the LORD,
for only he will release my feet from the
snare.

¹⁶ Turn to me and be gracious to me,
for I am lonely and afflicted.

¹⁷ Relieve the troubles of my heart
and free me from my anguish.

¹⁸ Look on my affliction and my distress
and take away all my sins.

¹⁹ See how numerous are my enemies
and how fiercely they hate me!

²⁰ Guard my life and rescue me;
do not let me be put to shame,
for I take refuge in you.

²¹ May integrity and uprightness protect
me,
because my hope, LORD, is in you.

²² Deliver Israel, O God,
from all their troubles!

my enemies will stumble and fall.

I have trusted in the LORD
and have not faltered.

² Test me, LORD, and try me,
examine my heart and my mind;

³ for I have always been mindful of your
unfailing love
and have lived in reliance on your
faithfulness.

⁴ I do not sit with the deceitful,
nor do I associate with hypocrites.

⁵ I abhor the assembly of evildoers
and refuse to sit with the wicked.

⁶ I wash my hands in innocence,
and go about your altar, LORD,

⁷ proclaiming aloud your praise
and telling of all your wonderful deeds.

⁸ LORD, I love the house where you live,
the place where your glory dwells.

⁹ Do not take away my soul along with
sinners,
my life with those who are
bloodthirsty,

¹⁰ in whose hands are wicked schemes,
whose right hands are full of bribes.

¹¹ I lead a blameless life;
deliver me and be merciful to me.

¹² My feet stand on level ground;
in the great congregation I will praise
the LORD.

Psalm 27

Of David.

¹ The LORD is my light and my salvation—
whom shall I fear?
The LORD is the stronghold of my life—
of whom shall I be afraid?

² When the wicked advance against me
to devour me,
it is my enemies and my foes
who will stumble and fall.

³ Though an army besiege me,
my heart will not fear;
though war break out against me,
even then I will be confident.

⁴ One thing I ask from the LORD,
this only do I seek:
that I may dwell in the house of the LORD
all the days of my life,

NOBODY

8/17

---

a Two Hebrew man
b The Hebrew has Selah
c This psalm is an acrostic poem, the ver

TURN YOUR MISTAKES INTO CONFETTI

I write pretty letters for a living, and I mess up every single day. Whether it is a letter that isn't as cute as I'd hoped, a splatter of ink, or a misspelled word, I am constantly casting aside pieces of colorful paper that don't quite make the cut. Very early on in my journey, I was too cheap to throw all this colorful card stock away, and I got the brilliant idea that I could turn my scrap paper into confetti.

I started running my bucket of "mess-ups" through my newly purchased office shredder, and out came the most beautiful confetti I'd ever seen! I was instantly hooked. When holding those colorful, textured, tiny pieces of paper, I could no longer see the individual mistakes that caused me to scrap it in the first place. When it was all mixed together, it was a masterpiece. I started sprinkling my homemade confetti into orders when people purchased my work online, and not only did it make them feel as if they were receiving a present, but it put smiles on their faces. Confetti is just trash, y'all. Those little bitty pieces were just my calligraphy trash living a happier life. I turn *all* my mistakes into confetti.

I believe I was put here on this earth to tell you that your mistakes can be made into confetti too—whether it's in your lettering or in your life! Your mess can be your message. God can use all the hard things, the mess-ups, the stories you don't love, and the parts you aren't proud of. None of it has to be perfect. It can still have a happy ending, and God can use our confetti for His glory if we'll let Him. I am living proof. Don't be sad when you mess up. It only helps you grow.

He has made everything beautiful in its time.
ECCLESIASTES 3:11 ESV

TURN YOUR mistakes INTO confetti

STEP 1

When composing this quote, I draw the big words first, so I started with "Mistakes" and "Confetti."

STEP 2

I go back in and add hand lettering downstrokes and shading to the word confetti since it's most important.

STEP 3

Lastly, I finish the quote by writing "turn your" and "into" in a block font so that they fit in between the other words.

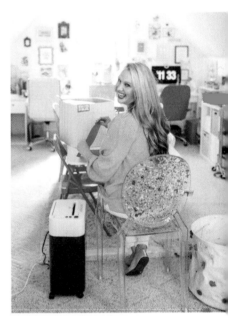

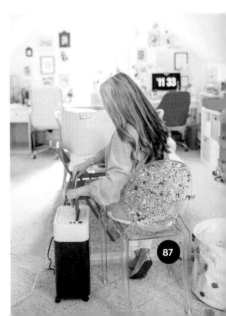

YOU ARE SO LOVED

*Beloved, let us love one another, for love is from God,
and whoever loves has been born of God and knows God.*
I JOHN 4:7 ESV

The main reason I love sharing my hand lettering is because it makes other people feel loved and appreciated. It makes friends feel like they were worth the extra time and effort it took me to write out something with a pen and then go over every letter a second and third time with extra care.

My love language is words of affirmation, so naturally a handwritten note of kind words is worth a thousand extra-credit points to me...but we can all use reminders that we are loved—by our families, our friends, ourselves (even if we are still working on that part), and, most importantly, by the Lord. God's love surrounds us, mistakes and all. He is never expecting the standard of perfection that the world seems to place on our shoulders. He didn't call us to be perfect; He called us to be good. Our best is plenty for Him. There isn't anything we can do to earn His love. God gives us His heart even when we don't deserve it.

For this project, I want you to write out the words "You are so loved" two separate times—one as a reminder for yourself and one as a gift to pass on to a friend.

The main words in this phrase are "You" and "loved," while "are so" are not as important. For this reason, I will choose to emphasize "You" and "loved" in my design and make "are so" a little less prominent. I will do this by mixing my Signature Swirl font with my Excited Caps style.

With new designs, it may take a couple of tries to lay it out the best way. Sometimes I sketch it out with a pencil, or I use my iPad, where it's easy to erase. Once I get a layout I love, I go straight to the paper with marker. You can try laying the practice paper underneath for spacing, but it's not really necessary. I don't *ever* recommend tracing over pencil lines you plan to erase later, though, because those marks won't disappear 100 percent.

To begin our project, I'll start with "You" and letter that with a capital *Y* in my Signature Swirl. Then I'll actually write "loved" next so that the two words will start to weave together like a puzzle. I love to intertwine words as much as possible, and the way to achieve that look is to sometimes write them out of order. I will come back after that and write "are so" in Excited Caps wherever they fit. Now, let's spread some love.

Trace the phase below. Remember, do the big words first ("you" and "loved") then fill in with the smaller words ("are so").

Trace the phrase below, add the lines, and shade it in. Then add your own print for the words "are so" between "you" and "loved."

GIFT TAGS AND GIFT BAGS

Your talent is God's gift to you. What you do with it is your gift back to God.
LEO BUSCAGLIA

My favorite thing to write is people's names.

Your name is your favorite word, whether you realize it or not. As a child, I looked high and low for a souvenir with "Maghon" emblazoned across it. I would have been happy with a pencil or a key chain, or maybe even a mug, but what I always wanted was one of those cool toy license plates with my name. I'm still on the hunt, by the way, if you ever find one. I think this is part of why I love creating personalized gifts for people. Taking the time to sit down and write the letters of a loved one's name can be such a special process. It's thoughtful and time-consuming in the best way, and it will make them feel cherished.

One of the easiest and most fun ways to use happy hand lettering skills is by lettering on gift tags and place cards! These instantly dress up packages and place settings with very minimal effort, and they can also serve as keepsakes for your friends and family. I save *all* of the hand-lettered gift tags and place cards I receive.

I love to purchase blank gift tags, but if you'd like a little more direction, I've included a template for cutting your own out of colorful card stock!

Practice some names on the tags below. Once you feel you get confortable, transfer your lettering onto real gift tags!

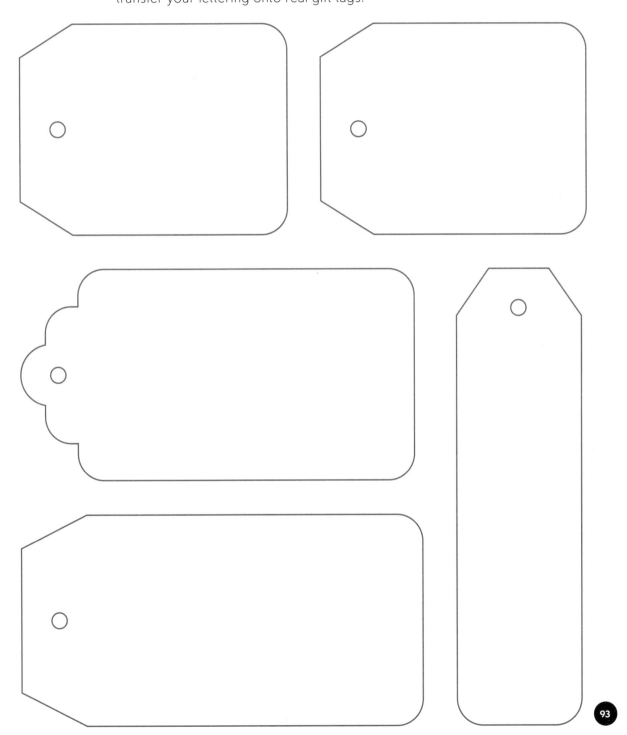

I take up as much room as possible on the front of the tag! I don't write the normal "to" and "from" on the front of the tag like most people. Instead I write their name as big as I can in my happy hand lettering. I start all the way on the far left side where I've placed the hole, and I let my design continue as large as it can be, all the way across to the right side—the bigger the better. My hope is that my gift tag will distract them from my terrible wrapping job (I use sticky bows and entirely too much tape) and delight them almost as much as the present itself.

Once I have the recipient's name drawn out, I go back over it to add my downstroke lines and shading to each letter (since I love them and they are totally worth the extra time and effort). I usually take a regular ink pen and add "Love, Maghon" in my grocery-list script on the back! Especially since I used up all of my efforts on their name. But it also helps to show the contrast and how special they really are since I spent so much more time on their name than on mine.

Another style I like to use for gift tags, especially if I am in a hurry, is what I like to call "the Price is Right"! Do you remember that TV show? I have the best memories of hearing it play in the background during my early childhood years. For this style, I use my Excited Caps and, again, take up as much space as possible. You can go back over it and add shading or leave it be, but either way it will scream, "COME ON DOWN! This gift is for you!" to your intended recipient.

The same technique can also be applied to gift bags! As I mentioned, I am not the world's best present wrapper, so I think the gift bag is the best invention since sliced bread. I buy a dozen blank gift bags and then use a gold paint pen to letter a name all across the front. This can be cute for baby or wedding showers too, because it's often the first time they will get to see the new name written out.

For baby showers, I will do "Baby Smith"— or if we know the name, "Sweet baby Harrison." Always mixing print and script fonts, whichever way looks best.

Weddings gift bags are fun because I write "the future" really small and Mrs. New Last Name huge because we all know that her new last name is what she really wants to see! When you decorate a gift bag, you don't really need a gift tag too, since everybody is going to be oohing and aahing at the gift table, asking, "Who wrote that gift bag!?" Or my personal favorite—"Well, we *know* who wrote that one!" (Insert humble shoulder shrug/wink here.)

Try a tag with print and a tag with script on these below. Which is your fave?

LET'S PRACTICE!

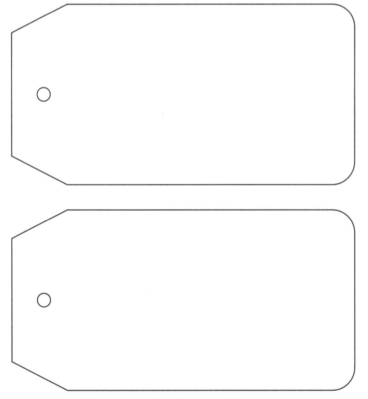

YOU ARE A LIGHT

Let your light shine before others,
so that they may see your good works and
give glory to your Father who is in heaven.
MATTHEW 5:16 ESV

In my sixth-grade quote book, I hand-lettered, "To the world you may be one person, but to one person you may be the world." Oh so dreamy! Funny enough, the guy I had in mind when I wrote that in middle school is the exact guy I went on to marry a hundred years later...but it's safe to say we took our sweet time figuring it out. I can't believe I am saying so, but this quote still stands true all these years later.

You are a light in this world to somebody in your life too. *You* are the best part of their day. It may be your roommate, a coworker, your son, daughter, grandparents, mom, or mail lady. Just think about it. Of *all* the people you encounter during any given day, you have the power to make their day brighter. Even in the smallest of ways: a shared smile, a laugh, a hug, a high five, or my personal fave—a surprise note tucked away for them to find later!

My Nana was the first artist I ever knew. She was amazingly talented as a painter. She painted everything from life-sized yard decorations for Christmas to the most intricate puffy-paint sweatshirts that everybody *had* to have back in the day. In a time before Etsy or selling your work on the Internet was even a thing, she was rocking and rolling! She called me "her sunshine," and that stuck with me. *You* are somebody's sunshine too. Right now, right this moment. Whether you're rocking a messy bun and sweatpants or whether you're feeling like it or not, you are. Don't think for a second that you need to dim your beautiful light in order for someone else to shine. You are a bright light in this world, and better yet, the brighter you shine, the more chances you have to extend that light to others. Lighting another person's candle doesn't diminish your own light—it just makes yours shine even brighter.

For this project, hand letter each phrase as a reminder that no matter your circumstances, you can choose to shine anyway. The world needs your light.

you are my
SUNSHINE

you
LIGHT UP
my LIFE

YOU ARE THE
BRIGHTEST
LIGHT

IN THIS WORLD

BLESSING OTHERS WITH YOUR GIFTS

If you want to do something nice for God,
do something nice for one of His kids.
BOB GOFF

Would you like to know my favorite "happiness hack"? If I wake up in a funk or have a stressful day, if I feel sleepy or just plain annoyed, guess what I do? I do something nice for somebody else. I live two miles from Starbucks, and the easiest and fastest way to cure my ailing heart is to hop in the car, jump into the drive-through line, and pay for the coffee of the car behind me. I pump upbeat music all the way there and all the way back...and even though I've done this almost every Friday for years, happy tears still flood my eyes as we pull away. It *always* does my heart good to do something good.

We were created to bless others with our gifts. BREAKING NEWS! Hand lettering is now one of your gifts! How can you use it to bless someone else?

Look for ways that you can spread joy by doing thoughtful things for others. Expressions of love and caring don't have to be huge or over-the-top to be meaningful. Here are some of my favorite quotes that I like to write out and give the workers in the drive-through to pass on to the next car when I'm spreading coffee (and kindness) like confetti!

THIS
is the day
THAT THE
Lord
HAS MADE

SPREADING HAPPINESS THROUGH YOUR HANDWRITING

You could hand letter and hang up encouraging messages on a bathroom mirror. You could volunteer to hand letter a friend's baby announcements since her hands are full. You could donate your skills to a local nonprofit for a new hand-lettered logo. You could share your happy hand lettering skills with a friend.

HAPPY MAIL ENVELOPES

*Let us consider how to stir up one another
to love and good works.*
HEBREWS 10:24 ESV

Speaking of sharing hand lettering skills with a friend...I *love* sending (and who are we kidding?—also receiving) happy mail.

When I go to my mailbox, I always open a handwritten piece first. Don't you? I am standing there sorting and thinking, "Junk mail, junk mail, catalog, coupon..." and then, "Yay, someone wrote me something!" At this stage in my life, it is usually a baby shower invitation or a thank-you note, but I am filled with joy nonetheless.

Right out of college I moved from North Carolina all the way to Southern California. Initially it was *so* cool to say I lived "just outside of LA" or that I could feast on In-N-Out daily and then bask in the sun, but I was far away from home and everybody who loved me. I was the saddest I had ever been in my life. I was ashamed and I was embarrassed and I felt like a failure. I tried to be strong. I tried to stick it out. But I knew it wasn't where I belonged, and I was losing myself more and more each day. Throughout my time there I found myself *so* looking forward to the mail each day. My mom knew how much I was struggling and would send cards that had made her think of me. Some had bright colors; some had glitter... And all of them had beautiful words of life that she saw fit to share with me. She made these store-bought cards extra special by writing notes of encouragement to me with her favorite Scriptures inside. I needed those words more than she could have ever imagined. I would flip through the mail and my heart would start beating faster as soon as I recognized her handwriting, because I knew that I would feel *so* much better in just a few minutes, after reading whatever was inside. I saved every one of them, and I still have them today. I can't always remember what they said, but I will never forget how they made me feel.

Not only is the card inside a gift, but an envelope can be just as special. Whether it's for a birthday party, Christmas card, or simple thank-you note, taking a few minutes to treat the envelope like gift wrap on a present will make your day—and theirs.

Here are a few of my favorite envelope designs for you to practice...and then, you guessed it! Your homework is to send some happy mail encouragement to someone who lives far away.

USEFUL TIPS FOR LETTERING ENVELOPES

- Try an all print block style if you're in a hurry!

- Try an all script style if you're feeling fancy.

- A mix of cursive and print is my usual go-to.

- Start lettering about halfway down an envelope, but make sure to leave room for a fun postage stamp.

- Break abbreviation "rules" sometimes.

- Unless this is for a formal event (like a wedding) you can shorten words like Boulevard, Street, Apartment (Blvd. St. Apt.) and State Names (N.C. instead of North Carolina) IF that helps you with your spacing. If you need to take up more space, then don't abbreviate, keep them long instead.

- Sort your address list alphabetically by city (not last name) since that's the most consistent part of the address. This will help you go faster!

- Write large horizontally from end to end if you have trouble centering. If you're done and you're still a little bit off center, add a flourish to balance it out.

- Use colorful markers to match your card or holiday theme.

- Add embellishments and decorations: sparkles, stars, confetti, banners, arrows, fun punctuation, etc.

- Keep numbers simple and readable.

- Put your return address on the back flap (I use a stamp).

- Add a little confetti and send it on it's merry way!

THE
Birthday Girl
2100 FIESTA AVENUE
celebration, CA 29120

COMPARISON IS THE THIEF OF JOY

For am I now seeking the approval of man, or of God?
Or am I trying to please man?
If I were still trying to please man, I would not be a servant of Christ.
GALATIANS 1:10 ESV

If you knew the story God was writing in your own life, you'd never compare yours to anyone else's. I saw this quote a few months back, and it stopped me in my tracks. We've all heard that comparison is the thief of joy, and it is *so* true. Comparison is the thief of everything. I wouldn't even be here today with a thriving business if I hadn't stopped comparing my work to others. Early on in my lettering career, I found myself comparing my letters to the seasoned script of more professional calligraphers and hand letterers online. I was comparing my beginning to their middle. They had been at this so much longer, yet I was expecting myself to have those same results pouring from my pen. I knew I could never have the confidence to continue if I didn't stop trying to live up to them.

How many times have you seen someone's life on social media and thought yours didn't live up? You're likely comparing your worst day to someone else's highlight reel. I am guilty of this too. Over the years, I have learned that happiness comes when I stop comparing myself to others. God's got this. Your story is so uniquely yours and crafted by design. The season you're in may not be your favorite right now; your lettering may still need work; there may be huge life events you're still waiting on...but take it from me, if you keep your eyes on your own paper and "you do you," you will be so much happier in the long run.

One of my favorite quotes is: "*When you love what you have, you have everything you need.*" Look around and take a minute to appreciate all the things you have that you *love.* Meaningful relationships, a job, a safe place to come home to, food on the table—maybe a hot pink Sharpie!

Of course God will come along in His time and bless you with far more than you can even imagine, but I am sure you can find things that are pretty great in the meantime.

Remember to draw the big word ("enough") first, then fill in with the small print ("I am").

QUOTES TO LETTER

For the phrase below, draw "everything" and hand letter it first, then add "I have" and "I need" in the block font, second.

I HAVE Everything I NEED

YOU ARE STRONG, BOLD, BEAUTIFUL, AND BRAVE

Therefore encourage one another and build one another up.
I THESSALONIANS 5:11 ESV

In case nobody has told you in a while, hear it from me: You are strong. You are bold. You are beautiful, and you are brave. I am a big fan of compliments. I love giving them; I love receiving them. I love that they are so simple, yet they can totally change a mood or boost the happiness of others. If a compliment pops into your head, it needs to pop out of your mouth. I believe it was laid on your heart for a reason. We all struggle with insecurities in one way, shape, or form, and you have no idea how much your words will mean to someone else when you say them. You don't know what kind of day she may be having, what struggles she's facing, or how many times she changed her outfit this morning just to feel confident enough to walk out of her house. If you think something nice, say it. Your words could be a lifeline to someone you didn't even know was drowning. *You* have the power to make someone happy with your words. Your beautiful words can speak life into complete strangers, and I pray that you will take it as a sign when you think them, that you need to speak them.

Some of us may be shy at receiving compliments, and I want to encourage you to take the compliments with a smile, say "thank you," and then zip it, sister. They are trying to *bless you* with their words! If my two-year-old tells me I look pretty, I *ooh* and *aah* and tell him, "Thank you, sweet baby! That's so nice of you to say!" But if a friend or a stranger says it, I am quick to shrug it off. We don't need to take away someone's blessing by disagreeing with them, by shrugging it off and saying "No, *you* are" or any other silly commentary that we quickly return. Thank them! Accept their praise and appreciate the fact that they saw something beautiful in you—that maybe you didn't even see in yourself.

We are all in this together. We need to come alongside our fellow mothers, sisters, daughters, and friends and offer a phrase of praise. Let's bless other women and lift them up instead of tearing them down. Giving and receiving compliments is such a small way of doing this, but spreading happiness doesn't have to be big to be important. Compliment someone today. I'll go first. I think you have great taste in books!

For this project, hand letter the powerful compliment and repeat it out loud to yourself:

you are STRONG Beautiful BOLD AND BRAVE

What are some other phrases you could speak into life?

What is a compliment that *you* need to hear?

Now, commit to sharing these kind words with friends and strangers. If you have the chance to make someone's day with your happy hand lettering, *do* it! Writing it is even better, because it can be read again and again!

Write a phrase below that you can share with a friend.

LET'S PRACTICE!

ALL GOOD DAYS

Trust in the LORD with all your heart,
and do not lean on your own understanding.
In all your ways acknowledge him,
and he will make straight your paths.
PROVERBS 3:5-6 ESV

I don't have very many bad days. It's not that hard things don't happen (they do), and it's not that everything goes my way (it doesn't), but I started comparing my bad moments to the worst moments of my life, and now none of them seem so bad. I actually think it's because I have survived hard times that I am able to appreciate the good times while I am blessed enough to live them.

Getting a speeding ticket is still terrible, but it's not as bad as being in a car accident. My child throwing a tantrum in Target is not fun, but neither was being afraid that I wouldn't ever be able to have a child in the first place. Losing your car keys isn't anywhere near as hard as losing your job. It's not that you aren't allowed to feel sadness or pain; of course you are. But I do my best to feel it, to acknowledge it, and then to move on and try to turn the day back around. This small shift in perspective helps keep me happy overall, even when my day may be heading off the rails. I ask myself, "Are you really having a bad day, or was it just a few bad hours?"

If this is the worst season of your life, I am so sorry. I have been there, and I can assure you that better days are ahead. I am living life on the other side of my worst days so far, and I praise God for them because they made me stronger in my faith, my confidence, and even my sense of self-worth. When we decide to put everything in God's hands, we will eventually see God's hands in everything.

If you're coming to the end of the day and you still feel weary or like you need to chalk this one up as a loss, tomorrow is a fresh start. We are blessed with a brand-new day and brand-new chances to try again. At the end of every day I sing a song to my son that I made up. It lists everyone in our family or what we saw that day and thanks the Lord for blessing us with another good day. It goes like this:

Vance Had a Good Day,
Vance Had a Good Day,
Vance Had a Good Day,
Thank You, thank You, Lord.

And then we repeat whoever he says (Mama, Dada, Granna, Poppie, Dog Dog, Lawn Mower, Golf Cart)! You never know what will come out, but we are quick to sing our praises.

There is hope and there are promises that God won't ever leave us—even during the hardest of times. My mom always said, "If God brings you to it, He will bring you through it!" It's going to be okay, okay? You have survived 100 percent of the worst days of your life. I believe in you. These are some of my favorite quotes that inspire me to make all of my days good days. I hope they will do the same for you!

New MORNING NEW Mercies

ALL good DAYS

YOUR NEW LIFE MOTTO

Gracious words are like a honeycomb,
sweetness to the soul and health to the body.
PROVERBS 16:24 ESV

If you change your words, you change your world. I hope by now you've seen that even spending just a few minutes writing and reading words of life can lift your spirits, boost your confidence, and make you a little bit happier than you were before. What if you could live by these words?

A few years ago I was doing some goal setting for myself and my business, and I found myself asking, "What words do you want to live by? What do you want to be known for? What do you want people to remember about you?" Here's what I wrote down:

That one little photo I shared (in my grocery-list script, by the way) has been shared hundreds of thousands of times, by Olympic gold medalists, reality TV stars, famous musicians, even Oprah's Pinterest account, and tons and tons of girls like you and me who are just trying to get by one day at a time. When I wrote out my own "life motto," as it came to be called, I never imagined the impact it would have. I thought it was just for me, but God had bigger plans. If I had known that many people would see it, I *definitely* would have hand lettered it instead. Hello!

WORK HARD

I wanted to put all my efforts into whatever job or task I was handed. I was raised in a family of hard workers, and I have always taken pride in my job. I wanted to give 110 percent at motherhood, marriage, work, and whatever circumstance I was facing. I wanted to try my best and not leave anything on the table.

> *Work willingly at whatever you do,*
> *as though you were working for the Lord*
> *rather than for people.*
> COLOSSIANS 3:23 NLT

STAY SWEET

I am the nice girl. Always have been, and always will try my best to be. No matter how much success I may have as a business owner or as an author, no matter what happens to me in my life, whether good or bad, I want to stay sweet. I want to stay true to myself, true to my roots, and always a little bit nicer than I need to be.

When I have a difficult customer or when I deal with the occasional Internet bully, I pray to stay sweet. Customer service can be a ministry in and of itself. My prayer is always that I will rise above and be kind to everyone, no matter what.

> *Be kind and compassionate to one another,*
> *forgiving each other,*
> *just as in Christ God forgave you.*
> EPHESIANS 4:32 NIV

TRUST GOD

This is the most important one for me. As I shared in the last project, I want God's hand in everything. I have tried it my way, and my life was a disaster. I want to pray about decisions, believe in His greater plan, and trust that when a door is closed, He has something so much better waiting on the other side. This is the hardest for me because sometimes I think that if I can just work hard enough or long enough, I can achieve anything. That's not true. I only want to work hard on the right things that God has planned for me in my life.

Trust in the LORD with all your heart
and lean not on your own understanding.
PROVERBS 3:5 NIV

LOVE DEEP

We are never going to run out of love, right? So I want to give away as much as I can. Before my husband and I started dating, I had my heart broken time and time again. I dated all the wrong guys and spent way too many years crying, praying, and hoping for things to work with each of them. Those unanswered prayers were the best blessing in the world for me. If even one of those relationships had worked, I wouldn't have his love in my life now. I never want to take my husband for granted, not for a single moment. I want to give as much love as I can to him and my son first, but since there's plenty of love to go around, there will be lots left to overflow to my family, friends, and the world. I want to love without fear of getting my heart broken. I want to love freely, without reservations, because God will always be there to restore me again and again.

Love never fails.
I CORINTHIANS 13:8 NIV

Did any of these phrases speak to you?

What words would you like to live by?

Is there a Scripture or a verse that you'd like to be reminded of daily?

What is your new life motto? Letter it below.   **NEW LIFE MOTTO**

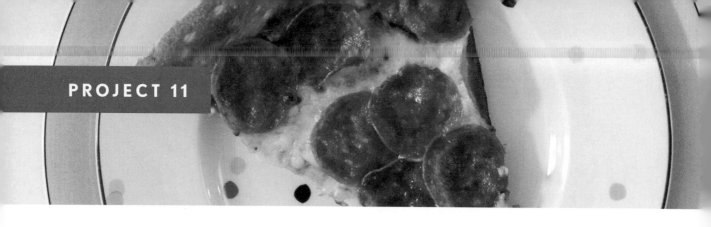

CELEBRATE EVERY DAY

This is the day that the LORD has made; let us rejoice and be glad in it.
PSALM 118:24 ESV

So often in life we save things for special occasions. We don't light candles unless company is coming over; we don't eat off the fancy plates; we save dresses in our closet until we get invited to a wedding. My husband and I started eating takeout pizza on our wedding china every Friday night when we were engaged. It was the perfect way to start the weekend and an awesome reminder that a moment doesn't have to be special to be celebrated. I don't want you to *save* your happy hand lettering skills for a special occasion. Life *is* a special occasion! We are so blessed to be here, able to enjoy little moments almost every day. Now, don't get me wrong—I live for holidays, but it's the little moments in between the big ones that really make a happy life. If you're always on the lookout for small ways you can indulge and celebrate, you will have so much fun!

One of my favorite ways to incorporate happy hand lettering into my everyday life is by lettering on my chalkboard that I've prominently placed on my front porch. I use sidewalk chalk to give her a fresh makeover every season or holiday. If we have a guest coming to stay with us, I will freshen it up with a welcome message. Nothing feels more like the Southern hospitality I was raised on than "Welcome, Minnie!" spelled out on our front porch. I also love adding a touch of lettering to our family wall calendar. Something as mundane as a vet appointment looks a lot more fun when I add some Signature Swirls.

What would you write if you had
a front porch chalkboard? Letter it below.

The holidays themselves abound with ideas to add happy hand lettering to your celebrations. Here are some of my favorite celebratory words and phrases to use all year round.

My trick when writing "Happy Everything" is that I write the holiday word first (for example, Halloween) in my Signature Swirl alFUNbet, and then I come back *after* I write the main word and add "Happy" in my Excited Caps. Adding "Happy" afterward gives better composition and helps make decorating easier.

Happy New Year
Happy Valentine's Day
Happy St. Patrick's Day
Happy Easter
Happy 4th of July
Happy Halloween
Happy Thanksgiving
Merry Christmas
Happy Fall Y'all

Happy Anniversary
Happy Birthday
Welcome
Mr. & Mrs.

FriYAY
Celebrate
Let's Party
Enjoy
Vacation

What are some of your favorite things to celebrate?

What are some nonholiday traditions you'd like to start?

What are some ways you can add happy hand lettering to your home?

LIVING ROOM	KITCHEN	BEDROOM	OTHER

GRATITUDE IS
THE BEST ATTITUDE

Consider it pure joy, my brothers and sisters,
whenever you face trials of many kinds,
because you know that the testing of your faith produces perseverance.
JAMES 1:2-3 NIV

If I could pinpoint one thing that makes me happier on a daily basis, hands down, it's gratitude. Sometimes I write all the things I'm grateful for in a journal (grocery-list script is just fine), and other times I list them when I say my prayers at night. I even made up a song that I sing to my son, Vance, every night, thanking God for each of us who had a good day (see project 9). In our home, you can find the word "grateful" in many different art forms all over our house. As soon as you walk through my door, it's the first thing you see in bold type, stenciled on a giant canvas. It's a reminder to be grateful in all circumstances, to remember the days we prayed for exactly the life we have now. In my All She Wrote Notes studio, as I am writing this the word "grateful" hangs above my head (covered in confetti, of course!).

Once you start listing things you're grateful for, you won't be able to stop. When I am making my gratitude lists, I find it gets overwhelming if I write down every little thing like house, car, electricity, water, etc. I am so fortunate to have those things, of course, but I enjoy my gratitude practice most when I write down ten things I am grateful for that happened *that day*. This makes me so happy. Once I know I'm going to list them, I start *looking* for things to be grateful for. I can't help it. As the saying goes, "A grateful heart is a magnet for miracles." It gives me a chance at the end of each day to reflect on the people, the moments, and the little things in my life that brought me joy.

When I go to bed every night with a grateful heart or, even better, start my day being thankful for every good thing that happened yesterday, I can't help but have a smile on my face.

Our next project is a list of gratitude. I want you to write a list of ten things you're grateful for that happened today (or yesterday). Challenge yourself to use the different fonts you've learned throughout this book. Signature Swirl, Excited Caps, and even grocery-list script is welcome here. Have *fun* with this, and it just may be something you want to continue again and again! I can't think of a more life-giving way to practice your happy hand lettering skills.

10 THINGS I AM GRATEFUL FOR TODAY

PROJECT 12: GRATITUDE IS THE BEST ATTITUDE

Here are some of my favorite quotes about gratitude. Remember, draw the big words first and hand letter them with steps 1, 2, and 3 (see page 35). Then add the print words second.

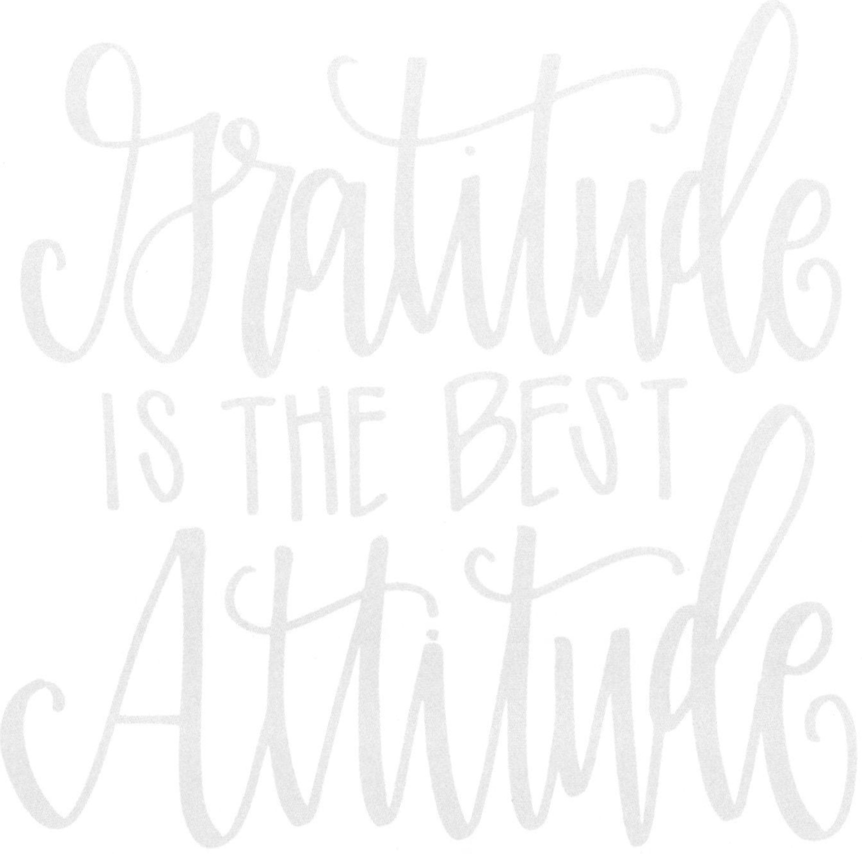

Gratitude
IS THE BEST
Attitude

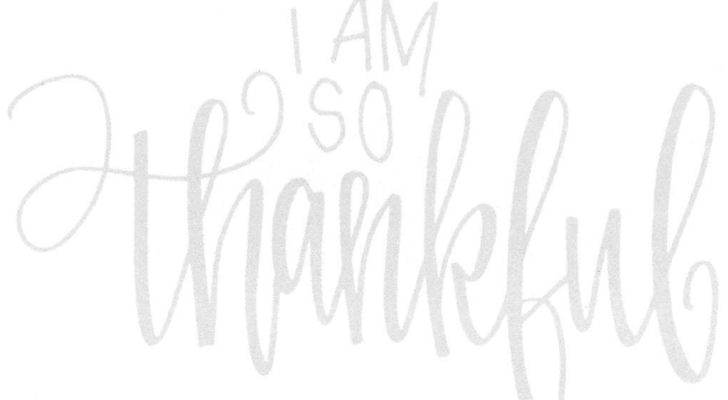

I AM
SO
thankful

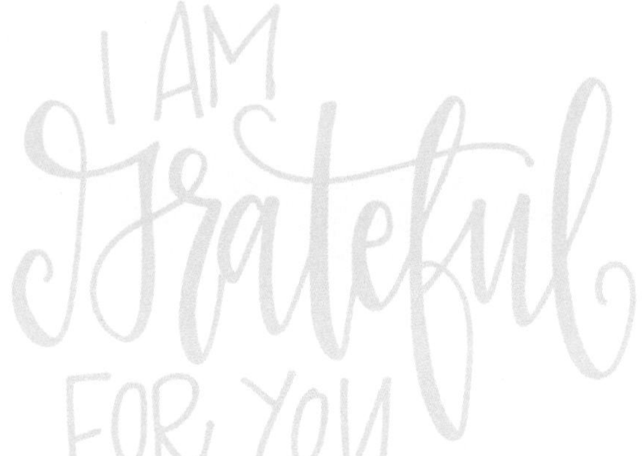

I AM
Grateful
FOR YOU

I REMEMBER THE
days I prayed
FOR WHAT I HAVE
NOW

gratitude
TURNS WHAT
WE have
INTO enough

THINKING OUTSIDE
THE BOX (OR PAGE)

*He has filled them with skill to do every sort of work done
by an engraver or by a designer or by an embroiderer in blue and purple
and scarlet yarns and fine twined linen,
or by a weaver—by any sort of workman or skilled designer.*
EXODUS 35:35 ESV

Reese Witherspoon is quoted as saying, "If it's not moving, monogram it"—and you can feel free to quote me, Maghon Taylor, as saying, "If it's not moving, hand letter on it!" I have taken this to the extreme on more than one occasion in our home. I wrote all over the back of an office chair, decorated a set of TV trays with "Celebrate every day," and emblazoned "Toss confetti" in sidewalk chalk on the wall in my office stairwell. In fact, I've used my favorite quotes in every home I've ever lived. I write on things with a Sharpie so often that my two-year-old son has caught on and he's taken his talents to the walls and the furniture. I can't even be mad, because deep down I am kind of impressed.

But, seriously, you can write on literally anything, so here are some fun ideas you can add to your seasonal celebrations featuring none other than your happy hand lettering.

PUMP-KALLIGRAPHY (FALL)

1. Use a real or faux pumpkin and start your word in the thickest ripple that you can find. Use a black paint marker or chisel tip Sharpie.

2. Take your time, drawing letter by letter, letting each letter stop to connect in between the ripples of the pumpkin as much as possible. Go back and add your thick lines to your **downstrokes**.

3. Keep your design contained to half of the pumpkin so that it is readable when facing forward. You can even add a second design on the back!

HOLI-YAY ORNAMENTS (WINTER)

1. Purchase the clear, fillable ornaments at your local craft store. I love choosing unbreakable ornaments whenever possible. However, if you choose to use the round glass ball ornaments, consider turning your lap desk upside down and use the bean bag portion on the back of it to rest your ornament in while writing on it. It really works wonders!

2. Use a paint marker such as a decocolor or a gold Sharpie marker. I love gold, but black or silver works great too!

3. Draw your letters one at a time and then come back and add thick lines to your **downstrokes**. I love writing one word like a name, family name, or Christmas-themed word like joy, hope, or love. Tie the ornament with a bow, add some confetti, and spread Christmas cheer far and near!

EGG-CELLENT EASTER EGGS (SPRING)

1. Purchase faux or real eggs and your favorite Sharpie markers. I use a fine point for faux eggs but an extra-fine point for real eggs.

2. I like displaying the eggs with the pointy end up. I reinforce the faux eggs with a piece of tape on the reverse side so that the halves don't fall apart and the names stay lined up. I hand letter the names and then go back and add thickness to my **downstrokes**.

3. For real eggs, you can also decorate them with colored markers of your choice, just be gentle! I wouldn't recommend eating them afterwards, just in case! These will make *EGG-cellent* place cards for Easter brunch and every *bunny* will be impressed!

FUN IN THE SUN FLOATS (SUMMER)

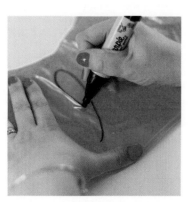  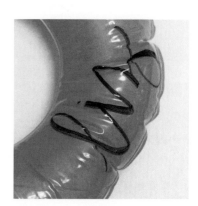

1. Use a chisel tip Sharpie marker and find the least wrinkly section of a deflated pool float.

2. Take your time, drawing letter by letter in either cursive or print script. Lettering should only take up about a quarter of the diameter of the float.

3. Go back and add thickened **downstrokes** to each letter. Let it dry. Inflate your float and hit the pool!

Use this space to practice placement
before lettering straight on your fun things!

DO ONE THING EVERY DAY
THAT MAKES YOU HAPPY

Delight yourself in the LORD, and he will give you the desires of your heart.
PSALM 37:4 ESV

What makes you happy? What fires you up? What gives you chills, makes you smile, cry happy tears, or get a warm, fuzzy feeling inside? These are little things. They don't have to cost money, but they are important. This is the best "happiness hack" I can offer you: find the little things in life that make you happy, and commit to doing more of those things every single day.

For me, it's bright colors. I feel *so* much better when I am wearing sunshine yellow, even if it's 40 degrees outside in January. I fully accept that I am a Fruit Loop™ in a world full of Cheerios™, but it brightens my day, and it actually brightens others' days too. When they see me coming, they smile. Well, they are either smiling or laughing, but I am good with it either way. Happy people tend to make other people happy too.

I always remember my Nana having her nails painted pink. I don't love typing on the computer (you're welcome, by the way) so I paint my nails hot pink because it makes me happier when I'm typing if I am watching those beauties dance across my rainbow-colored keyboard (another happiness booster). I light candles every day instead of saving them for when company is coming over. I listen to upbeat music. I love swinging on my porch, and I get outside even if it's just to walk to the mailbox. I love listening to my little boy laugh hard, and I love when my husband gives me a big hug and a forehead kiss when he leaves for work. It makes me happy when Gracie or Teddy (our dogs) cuddle up next to me on the couch. I love a good podcast, a great sermon, and relaxing in a bubble bath until the water gets cold. I love encouraging other women, spreading positivity, paying it forward, and, of course, I love doodling, drawing, crafting, or any pursuit of creativity.

What does "happy" look like for you? Puppy snuggles, baby giggles, warm popcorn? I want you to make a list—right here, right now! Use your skills; make it fun and pretty. And then I want you to cut it out and tape the list somewhere you can see it. When your day is heading off the rails or when you're feeling like you need a boost, choose *one* thing off of your list and go do it right away. And then the next day, add two things. Before you know it, you'll have *all sorts* of happy moments throughout your day. It really is the little things. All the tiny moments add up to big joy before you know it. A happy day is made up of happy moments, and a happy life is filled with happy days.

You know all those things that make you happy? What are you waiting for? You should go do them.

PROJECT 14: DO ONE THING EVERY DAY THAT MAKES YOU HAPPY

Now that you have seen my happy list, make a list of your own below. Then on the next page (page 141), hand letter your happy list, tear it out of the book, and place it somewhere as a reminder to do one at least one thing every day that makes you happy!

HAPPY

THE PARTY
DOESN'T HAVE TO STOP

There's confetti on the floor and the DJ is playing the last song, but our party together doesn't have to end. I can't wait to see how you use your happy hand lettering. If you don't remember anything else from our time together, remember to turn your mistakes into confetti—in life or in lettering. It doesn't have to be perfect to be happy. If you have the chance to make someone else happy, you won't ever regret taking it.

These letters are the little things that we can use to make our mark on the world—a mark that just so happens to look a lot more fun in a hot pink Sharpie, right? This is a new way to add more joy, to create more happy moments for ourselves and our loved ones, to feel creative again when we've spent all day looking at a screen. This is your reminder to choose beautiful words of life every chance you get and to bless others with your newfound gifts.

I am so grateful to you for buying this book and learning along with me. I sincerely hope it made you smile. None of this was my plan, but that's the thing about God—His plans are always *far* greater than we can ever imagine. Thank you for helping me spread happiness through my handwriting.

And that's all she wrote!

let's be FRIENDS

@ALLSHEWROTENOTES ON INSTAGRAM

ALL SHE WROTE NOTES ON FACEBOOK

SHOP: ALLSHEWROTENOTES.COM

LEARN ONLINE: HAPPYHANDLETTERING.COM